A Free Heart

VONETTE Zachary BRIGHT

NewLife PUBLICATIONS

My Heart in His Hands Bible Study: A Free Heart

Published by
NewLife Publications
A ministry of Campus Crusade for Christ
P.O. Box 620877
Orlando, FL 32862-0877

ISBN 1-56399-179-9

Design and production by Genesis Group

Cover by Koechel-Peterson Design

Printed in the United States of America

Unless otherwise indicated, Scripture quotations are from the *New International Version*, © 1973, 1978, 1984 by the International Bible Society. Published by Zondervan Bible Publishers, Grand Rapids, Michigan.

For more information, write:
Campus Crusade for Christ International—100 Lake Hart Drive, Orlando, FL 32832, USA

L.I.F.E., Campus Crusade for Christ—P.O. Box 40, Flemington Markets, 2129, Australia

Campus Crusade for Christ of Canada—Box 529, Sumas, WA 98295

Campus Crusade for Christ—Fairgate House, King's Road, Tyseley, Birmingham, B11 2AA, United Kingdom

Lay Institute for Evangelism, Campus Crusade for Christ—P.O. Box 8786, Auckland, 1035, New Zealand

Campus Crusade for Christ—9 Lock Road #3-03, PacCan Centre, Singapore

Great Commission Movement of Nigeria—P.O. Box 500, Jos, Plateau State, Nigeria, West Africa

My Dear Friends

I want to welcome you to this Bible study series for women! I'm excited about the opportunity to walk through the Scriptures with you as we explore all that God's Word has for the busy woman of today.

Every unique detail of a woman's life fits into a grand and glorious plan. My prayer is that women of all ages will desire to have a deeper relationship with God, and to discover the joys of knowing Him and His plan for their lives.

God's Word speaks so directly to every aspect of a woman's life. It fills us with wisdom, imparts God's love, and provides ample instructions for our daily walk. The Scriptures tell us the results we can expect when we live in agreement with God's plan, and what we can expect if we do not live as He directs.

The Bible has much to say about its value and relevance for our lives today. It gives us guidance: "Your word is a lamp to my feet and a light for my path" (Psalm 119:105). It gives understanding: "The unfolding of your words gives light; it gives understanding to the simple" (Psalm 119:130). It is not made up of cold, dead words, but living, Spirit-filled words that can affect our hearts and our lives: "For the word of God is living and active. Sharper than any double-edged sword, it penetrates even to dividing soul and spirit, joints and marrow; it judges the thoughts and attitudes of the heart" (Hebrews 4:12).

When I wrote the devotional books for the series *My Heart In His Hands*, it was with the desire to encourage women and to help them realize that God is interested and involved in the details of their lives. My goal was to provide a practical and systematic way for a woman to examine her heart and recognize how beautifully God has created her. This set of study guides has been designed to complement each seasonal devotional.

Each study guide has been developed prayerfully and can be used for individual or group study. Perhaps you are part of a group that meets regularly to study and discuss the precious treasures of God's Word. I have been a part of such groups for many years, and I am still overjoyed to meet with these women.

Whether you will study on your own or with others, it is my heartfelt prayer that you will open your heart to His Word and enjoy the blessing of resting confidently in His hands.

From my heart to yours,

Vonette Z. Bright

How to Use This Study

The *My Heart in His Hands* Bible study series is designed for the busy woman who desires a deeper walk with God. The twenty lessons in *A Free Heart* embrace the glorious truth that any Christian woman can live a victorious lifestyle—no matter what life throws in her path.

A Free Heart provides everything you need to understand biblical principles and use them to transform your life. Whether you are working hard at your career, involved in full-time ministry, knee-deep in preschoolers, or raising teenagers, you can find the time to complete the short lessons and receive encouragement for your day. The questions require less time than most courses so that you can fit Bible study into your hectic schedule. The refreshing look at Scripture passages will help you apply God's Word to your daily needs.

You can use this book as an individual study during your quiet time with God, or as a group study with other women. (A Discussion Guide with answers to the Bible questions is located at the back of this book to help a group facilitator.) It can also be used as a companion to the *My Heart in His Hands* devotional series.

The book contains an in-depth look at the lives of two women: a biblical portrait of a godly woman and an inspirational portrait of an outstanding contemporary woman. These portraits, woven throughout the book, give insights into a free heart.

Each lesson includes these parts:

- His Word—a Scripture passage to read
- Knowing His Heart—understanding God's Word
- Knowing My Heart—personal questions to consider
- My Heart in His Hands—a timely quote to ponder

Whether to start your morning or end your day, you can use this study to focus on God's Word and on His marvelous works in your life. As you apply these principles, you will truly discover a free heart!

What It Means to Be Free

One of the words we hear most frequently in America is "free." Open up any newspaper and you will see the word emblazoned across all kinds of ads:

"Buy one, get one free!"

"Free interest for one year!"

"Free gift with any purchase!"

Have you ever had to explain to your children why the items advertised as "free" aren't really free? There are strings attached. The customer usually must buy something to get the "free" item —which stretches the concept of getting something for free.

However, when a store does truly offer something free, people are immediately attracted to it. At one point during the energy crisis of the 1970s, a gas station began giving away free gas. Cars were lined up for miles in front of that station.

In so many ways, people are fooled into thinking they are getting something for "free" when they are not. The criminal who avoids a jail sentence due to a technicality is physically free, but what about his freedom from guilt? The person who shoplifts doesn't have to pay for the items at the moment, but in time will likely get caught. The person who has "free" sex may end up with a venereal disease or an unwanted pregnancy and certainly emotional baggage.

Worry and guilt are two of the obstacles that keep us from having a free heart. The writer of the comic strip "Cathy" puts her finger on how tied up we are in our own guilty consciences.

Cathy is constantly feeling guilty about being overweight, so she eats low-calorie, low-fat foods. But she ends up eating so much of these good-for-you foods that she consumes more calories than she would have if she'd eaten regular foods. Then Cathy worries about the additives in the low-calorie foods and what they are doing to her body. Of course, trying on a swimsuit in the clothing store accentuates her worries.

What is keeping you from having a free heart? Financial worries? Feelings of inadequacy as a parent? Personal demands to have high standards for yourself? The burden of keeping your home spotless? Work-related conflicts? Aging concerns?

Many influences contribute to our feelings of being weighed down. For example, television commercials accentuate minor flaws to propel viewers into buying a product. In one ad, a woman is so devastated about a cold sore on her lip that she hides her face from her coworkers. Then she finds the medical "cure" and her cold sore heals. Only at this point does she feel she can face her friends. The moral? She has been "freed" from her cares because she looks perfect once more.

Isn't that a sad commentary on how we let temporary matters rob us of our freedom? We live in the freest society on earth yet have some of the heaviest hearts on the planet. Why is this? Because political, emotional, or any other temporal freedom doesn't bring lasting peace of mind.

In this series of lessons, we will discover what true freedom is and how to obtain it. This freedom does not come from outward circumstances but rather from conditions of the heart. Only Jesus Christ can free our hearts.

Just as with any privilege, responsibilities follow. Once we understand the secret of how to have a free heart, we must consider the responsibilities of this great gift and how to live within the boundaries of our freedom.

The Heart of Mary Magdalene

When you hear the name Mary Magdalene, no doubt your mind recalls the woman she was, not the woman she became. I remember as a teenager being asked to play the part of Mary Magdalene in an Easter pageant. I refused the part because I knew I would be teased about being demon-possessed. I could not see beyond her former state to the honor and privilege she had of being the first person to view the resurrected Christ.

Although the Gospels mention Mary Magdalene by name more than any other female disciple, none of the Scripture references tell us of her life before Jesus healed her. Yet, because Jesus cast seven demons out of her, we can imagine what a dark life of desperation she led. But Jesus Christ looked beyond the wild-eyed insanity of the demon-possessed woman, and, with love and compassionate authority, commanded the tormenting demons to come out—and stay out! Just think of how her face must have looked when she was freed from the terrible bondage of the spirits that distorted every dimension of her life!

From that moment, Mary led a life of surrender and commitment to Jesus and was a loving, enthusiastic follower. Not only did she accompany Jesus while He was popular, but she also stuck by Him after He was arrested. When the religious leaders demanded His blood, she remained faithful to the One who had redeemed her life. She witnessed His death on the cross and watched the Roman soldier thrust his spear into her Savior's side.

A famous painting in the Louvre depicts the night of the crucifixion. Its caption reads: "The world is wrapped in shadow; the stars are dead; and yet in the darkness is seen a kneeling form. It is Mary Magdalene with loving lips and hands pressing against the bleeding feet of Christ." She not only was there through all the suffering, she tenderly helped prepare His body for burial.

On the third day after His death, while she was at His tomb, she heard Jesus speak to her, "Woman, why are you crying?" (John 20:13). Her broken heart was the first to witness resurrection power. First Jesus had freed her from the bondage of Satan, and now He freed her from the bondage of grief. It was a joyful freedom that energized her as she ran to tell the disciples about Christ's resurrection.

Mary Magdalene represents the powerful truth of God's grace as given in Matthew 10:8, "Freely you have received, freely give." God freely gave us His Son, and His Son freely gives us life. A freed, delivered Mary Magdalene never looked back to rehearse her bondage, but with a grateful heart devoted her life to serving Jesus.

Experiencing true freedom from our past represents one aspect of grace; extending that same measure of grace to others is the appropriate response. When you understand what Jesus has done to free you from the power of sin, you will want to share the news with others. You cannot give spiritual freedom to anyone, but, like Mary Magdalene, you can out of a heart of gratitude tell others what Christ has done for you and invite them to experience the true freedom that only He can give.

The Heart of Ethel Wilcox

What would you give to assure your freedom? Few of us have had to face that question as Ethel Wilcox did—and what she sacrificed was very precious to her. She was the single mother of one son. When he was still a teenager, he joined the military and became a jet pilot in Korea where he flew dangerous missions over enemy territory. In her book, *Power for Christian Living,* she describes a portion of a wonderful letter he wrote home: "As I fly over enemy territory in the blackness of the midnight hour, I have perfect peace. I am not afraid, for my complete trust is in Him."

Her next statement provides a glimpse into her own deep faith: "That night as he completed his mission, he finished the work God had for him to do. Although he was reported 'missing in action' here, he was present with the Lord over there.

"What comfort those words penned in that last letter brought to his loved ones as they, by the power of the indwelling Spirit, were enabled to give the sacrifice of praise, the fruit of the lips."

How could she praise God when she had just given up her only child for the cause of freedom in a country halfway around the world? When her son enlisted in the military, she probably was not prepared to face his sudden death. Once she received the dreaded news, she experienced the painful price of political freedom. Yet she still had her personal freedom that came from her heart, which trusted God in everything.

Ethel Wilcox understood what true freedom really means, and her contagious attitude influenced many people. An attractive woman with a very warm, effective teaching style, she presented the truth of God's Word in such a manner that people understood how to live a victorious life and enjoy the freedom that the abundant life offers. For twenty-five years, she served on the faculty of Northwestern College and produced her own radio programs. Those who knew her commented on her strength and commitment to the truth of God's Word. She was associated with Campus Crusade for Christ as a special representative and greatly influenced my life. One of the songs common in her day was *Let the Spirit of Jesus Be Seen in Me*. Ethel lived her life as an example of what it means to allow the Holy Spirit to be in control. She focused on the importance of "being" rather than "doing." Her faith was not controlled by a list of do's and don'ts, but by the indwelling power of the Holy Spirit.

Experiencing true freedom allows a woman to project the love and joy of Christ to those around her. Ethel could not have known that years after her death she would still have an influence through those who learned from her. Those she taught continue to share the excitement of what it means to die to self and to allow Christ to rule their hearts and minds.

When you put aside your agenda and live every day with the anticipation of whatever Christ brings into your life, you will be able to embrace freedom with confidence and joy. As you do, you will be certain to influence those who know you.

PART 1

Spiritual Freedom

One word that strikes fear in the hearts of people today is "terrorist." For Gracia and Martin Burnham, that word became very familiar. For 376 days, they and several others were held captive by the Abu Sayyaf terrorist group, which has ties to Al-Qaeda. The two New Tribes missionaries spent more than a year on the run in the Philippine jungles, sleeping in tents and facing gun battles.

Yet Martin and Gracia were freer than their captors. They displayed a heart of love toward the brutal terrorists who had already executed one hostage. They shared with their captors the care packages of food they received, and Martin never complained when forced to carry supplies. Each night for more than a year Martin sang Gracia to sleep to comfort her. And each night he was chained to a tree so that he could not escape. Invariably, he said "thank you" to the man who chained him.

On June 7, 2002, the day the Filipino Scout Rangers discovered the terrorist camp, Martin and Gracia were holding each other in a rare time when he wasn't chained to a tree. Martin told her, "The Bible says to serve the Lord with gladness. Let's go out all the way. Let's serve Him all the way with gladness." Then they prayed together and quoted Scripture to each other.

When the gun battle erupted, Gracia was wounded in the leg, but Martin suffered a gunshot in the chest. He went home to be with the Lord he loved so much.

How could anyone feel free enough, amid such danger and depravation, to love his captors daily and sing to his wife every night? How could Gracia, who lost her husband and suffered deeply, say at her homecoming in Rose Hill, Kansas, "We want everyone to know that God was good to us every single day of our captivity"? Because the only true freedom is that which God gives us through His Spirit. This freedom doesn't depend on circumstances but is produced by a loving God within the hearts of His children.

Jesus Christ provided spiritual freedom for us when He died on a cross to purchase us with His blood and to deliver us from Satan's kingdom. This was the greatest sacrifice in the history of the universe.

As believers, our lives are held in God's hand. The One who sent His Son to die for us will not leave us to fend for ourselves. We have gained a freedom that no one can take away—not even those who would hurt us physically, mentally, or emotionally.

In our first five lessons, we will examine the freedom that Christ has purchased for us and how it impacts the way we live. We will discover how we, too, can have the depth of freedom that Martin and Gracia experienced in a terrorist camp.

LESSON 1

Freely Provided

The beauty of a surprise party is that it is given out of love from a friend's heart. The party details are planned just to please the honored one. God planned a grand event for us too—our spiritual birthday, the moment we became His child. Even before the earth was created He laid out the plan, which involves His grace overflowing on our behalf. At the right moment, He sent His Son, Jesus Christ, to die on a cross to make the way for each of us to be reconciled to God through the forgiveness of our sin. Christ's blood purchased our spiritual freedom. It is the foundation for all other human freedoms. God's grace through Christ is a free gift—to you and me!

His WORD: Romans 5:15–17

KNOWING His HEART

1. Compare the roles of Adam and Jesus in our human condition.

2. What is meant by the paradox "through death came life"?

3. How do we receive God's gift of life? (See 2 Timothy 1:8–10.)

4. What are the benefits you received through grace (Romans 6:22)?

KNOWING *My* HEART

1. Restate Romans 6:23 in your own words.

2. Describe the freedom you have as a result of receiving God's gift of salvation through faith in Jesus.

3. What does it mean to you that, before time began, God planned to extend grace freely?

4. How would you describe this gift of grace to an unbelieving friend?

My HEART IN *His* HANDS

"Certainly, [eternal life] is the most expensive gift ever given, for it cost Jesus Christ His life."

—WARREN WIERSBE

LESSON 2

Freely Forgiven

In 1977, Julian and an accomplice broke into Mary Stein's home. They beat the 73-year-old to death with a piece of wood. As she was dying, she cried, "Oh, Lord, I'm coming home!" These words burned into Julian's mind. A year later, he placed his trust in Christ. God's Spirit began to work in his heavy heart and seventeen years after the crime, Julian confessed to the police. Today, he's serving a prison sentence for murder, but his heart is free. One of the greatest freedoms we can experience is forgiveness of sin—freedom from both the eternal punishment for sin and from the day-to-day burden of sin. God provides this freedom by forgiving us through Christ's death on the cross. He leads us to freedom by convicting us of our sin so that we will confess it.

His WORD: Romans 6:15–23

KNOWING His HEART

1. What is our condition before we know God?

2. What is our condition when we wholeheartedly obey God?

3. What does Psalm 103:11,12 tell us about our confessed sins?

4. How does 1 John 1:9 relate to our freedom from sin?

KNOWING *My* HEART

1. Contrast your feelings when you sin and when you confess that sin to God.

2. In what ways does a sin such as lying turn a person into its slave?

3. How has God's Spirit freed you from a particular sin habit?

4. Since God forgives us freely, what must we do when others hurt us?

My HEART IN *His* HANDS

"Forgiveness is the fragrance the violet sheds on the heel that has crushed it."
—MARK TWAIN

LESSON 3

The Boundaries of Freedom

As Americans, we believe that we are free to do as we please. But our freedom is relative. A person driving down a freeway during high traffic hours will not experience complete freedom. The car must be steered between the white lines at a speed that prevents the car from either rear-ending the vehicle in front or impeding traffic behind. For our own safety, there are limits to what we can do with our own bodies. Our homes must be built within certain specifications. Limits are present in spiritual freedom too. God has allowed us freedom—within certain boundaries. Staying within God's boundaries, like staying within the white lines on the freeway, keeps us safe and joyful. Straying outside the boundaries will cause a disaster.

His **WORD:** James 1:22–25

KNOWING *His* **HEART**

1. What shows us our boundaries and what should be our response (verse 22)?

2. What is the result of not doing what it says (verses 23,24)?

3. What happens if we act according to God's Word (verse 25)?

4. How do Jesus' words in John 8:31,32 apply to our freedom through God's Word?

KNOWING *My* HEART

1. Give one example of how God's Word has freed you.

2. Describe a time when you looked into God's Word but ignored what it says.

3. How are you searching God's Word and applying it to your life?

4. What new boundary do you need to set in your life to better conform to God's standard?

My HEART IN *His* HANDS

"Absolute truth belongs to Thee alone."
—GOTTHOLD EPHRAIM LESSING

LESSON 4

The Freedom of Grace

A little boy desperately wanted to carry a heavy box of his belongings from the garage into his bedroom. But when he tried to lift the box, it was too heavy for his small arms. His father asked if he needed help. "Just a little," the boy answered. The father helped the boy lift the box and carry it up the stairway. The son had one hand on the box while the father carried most of the weight. When they got the box to his room, the little boy said, "Thanks, Dad. All I needed was just a bit more muscle." Then he flexed his own arms to show how strong he was. The father chuckled, but said nothing. That's how God is with us. In His grace, He provides the strength for all we do. All we have to do is put our hand out and rely on His strength.

His **WORD:** Ephesians 2:1–10

KNOWING *His* HEART

1. According to verses 8 and 9, how do we receive salvation?

2. What part, then, do good works play in our life (verse 10)?

3. How do we gain access to the grace that allows us to have peace with God (Romans 5:1,2)?

4. What does Paul say is another result of God's grace (2 Corinthians 12:9,10)?

KNOWING *My* HEART

1. What difference will it make in your life if you rely on God's grace for strength rather than on your own strength?

2. Why do most believers try to serve God in their own strength?

3. Which aspects of your ministry give you the most difficulty?

4. How can you rely on Christ's power rather than your own strength in these areas?

My HEART IN *His* HANDS

"God can propose absolute liberty to the one in whom He is so working that the innermost choice is only that which He wills for him . . . There is no other freedom in the world but this."

—LEWIS SPERRY CHAFER

The Joy of Spiritual Freedom

Mary Magdalene's life is a study of contrasts between slavery and freedom. Before she met Jesus, she was bound much worse than even the Gadarene demoniac—she was inhabited by multiple evil spirits. Her chains of affliction, however, are not unlike the chains we all wore before we met Christ. Mary probably felt she had no way to extricate herself from her life of torment. Then she met the Lord and was liberated! Matthew and Luke record that she was delivered of seven demons. Just imagine how she must have felt when she believed in Jesus and He set her free! As a result, she became an avid disciple of Jesus. She saw Him perform miracles. She heard Him teach. She fellowshipped with other believers. And she witnessed His death and resurrection.

His WORD: Matthew 27:45—28:10

KNOWING *His* HEART

1. According to Luke 8:1–3, what was Mary's response after Jesus cured her of evil spirits?

2. What is so amazing about her actions in Matthew 27:55,56?

3. What does this say about her faithfulness to Christ?

4. What was her reward for her faithfulness (John 20:10–18)?

KNOWING *My* HEART

1. How were you like the former Mary Magdalene before you met Christ and received God's forgiveness?

2. What does freedom from the penalty of sin mean to you?

3. Why do you think the resurrected Lord chose to speak to Mary Magdalene first?

4. What is our responsibility because of our freedom in Christ (John 20:18)?

My HEART IN *His* HANDS

"No other system, ideology, or religion claims a free forgiveness and a new life to those who had done nothing to deserve it but deserve judgment instead."

—JOHN STOTT

PART 2

Created to Be Free

Y ou may be familiar with the movie *Free Willy*, the story of a black-and-white killer whale that lived in an aquarium for most of his life. A little boy, along with his family and friends, set out on an adventure to free Willy so that he could live in the ocean, free of his captors. The highlight of the movie was when Willy jumped over a barrier and swam out to meet his new friends in the Pacific.

There is a real-life Willy, an orca named Keiko who was captured off the shores of Iceland twenty-two years ago. He has lived in captivity since he was two years old, performing in aquatic parks and starring in movies.

In 1999, he was "freed." Trainers took him from his enclosure in Klettsvik Bay in Vestmannaeyjar, Iceland, to a nearby area where orcas feed. Since then, they have taken Keiko on dozens of "ocean walks" so he can socialize with other orcas, but he always returns to the boats. So far, he has not opted for "freedom" and to live with his kind. In the meantime, it takes $3 million a year to train Keiko to return to the wild and to care for him.

Many people are committed to giving Keiko his freedom, yet there is a good chance that Keiko is unable to live freely. Scientists think other orcas will not accept Keiko because he doesn't have the right mannerisms to show he is part of the "family."

We, too, were created to be free. In the Garden of Eden, Adam and Eve were free of guilt, free to do what was right, living in close communion with God. And then they sinned. Consequently, they lost their home in the garden and their close fellowship with God was broken.

All of us were outside the family of God until we accepted His forgiveness by trusting in His Son, Jesus. Through grace, God provided a way for us to join His spiritual family. But even when we receive this privilege, we still don't have the right "behavior" that makes family living exciting. We may have sin habits and continue to wrestle with our sin nature. But God has a solution for this problem, too. His Spirit, who lives within us, will teach us and enable us to live God's way.

Many times we try to go back to where we once lived—in sin. Just as Keiko followed the boats back to shore, we get involved in activities that alienate us from the free life God has given us. In these lessons, we will study ways we can learn how to live in God's family, according to His rules, with His Spirit's help. This will enable us to live freely, to grow spiritually, to become what God wants us to be.

We begin by studying our free will and how it affects our lives. Then we will tackle the problems of suffering, anxiety, anger, and our past. We will discover the warnings God's Word gives us about these areas that can bind our lives.

Free Will

It is amazing to me that God has given us a free will. If we look at any daily newspaper, we can see the results of human choice—abortion, theft, child abuse, divorce, murder, cheating, anger, hate, selfishness. The list of evil decisions is endless. But when people choose God's way, the results are supernatural: peace, joy, contentment, selflessness. God didn't create us to serve Him out of mere duty, but rather with a heart of love because of His love for us. When our choices are made in love, we are willing to accept whatever He has for us to do and experience. Even when we make wrong decisions, God waits for us to repent of our actions and do things the right way!

His **WORD:** Exodus 32:1–26

KNOWING *His* HEART

1. What were the reasons the Israelites chose idol worship (verses 1,25)?

2. What choice did Moses give the people when he saw what they had done (verse 26)?

3. What was Joshua's response to this choice (Joshua 24:15)?

4. How does James urge us to make this same choice (James 4:7)?

KNOWING *My* HEART

1. How does Isaiah 1:19 apply to your life today?

2. What difficult choice are you currently facing?

3. What might result from making this choice God's way?

4. What are the ultimate outcomes of choosing to follow God's will as a way of life?

My HEART IN *His* HANDS

"God of all goodness, grant us to desire ardently, to seek wisely, to know surely and to accomplish thy holy will, for the glory of thy name."

—THOMAS AQUINAS

LESSON 7

Freedom in Suffering

At some time in our lives, all of us will suffer in some way. This is a fact of life. But how we respond to suffering will make all the difference. God does not leave us without comfort or help. He is always waiting to undergird us, to give us wisdom through our trials, to teach us more about His love and His plan for our lives through our challenges. Yet as women, we sometimes let our circumstances overwhelm us and make us spiritually impotent. We either wallow in a pity party, give up in despair, or ignore what God is teaching us. This makes the experience of suffering valueless in our lives. Instead, we should view suffering as an opportunity to draw closer to God and to serve Him with a deeper understanding.

His WORD: 2 Corinthians 1:3–11

KNOWING *His* HEART

1. What will God do for us in times of suffering (Isaiah 43:2)?

2. How does 2 Corinthians 1:3–11 bear this out?

3. What is the instruction given in verse 4?

4. How should we respond in times of suffering (1 Peter 4:19)?

KNOWING *My* HEART

1. How has God walked with you through trying times?

2. How can Psalm 62:8 help you in times of pressure and suffering?

3. Why is it so important to comfort others even while you are suffering?

4. In what ways can Paul's experience of suffering encourage you?

My HEART IN *His* HANDS

"Pain and suffering are the dark strands through the tapestry of your life, providing the shadows that give depth and dimension to the masterpiece God is fashioning within you."

—JOSEPH F. GIRZONE

LESSON 8

Freedom from Anxiety

As a new believer, Angie was caught up in a lifestyle of worrying. She worried about driving on the freeway, getting good grades in graduate school, maintaining her relationship with her boyfriend, getting along with her parents. One Sunday, her pastor preached on the sin of worry. She began to cry during the service, realizing that her patterns of thinking were displeasing to God. But how could she change a way of life she had practiced since childhood? Breaking a thought habit like anxiety is impossible in our human strength. Only God can release us from the cares that drag us down. He promises us an abundant life whether we are living lives of comfort or hardship.

His **WORD:** Matthew 6:25–34

KNOWING *His* **HEART**

1. What are we commanded to do in verses 25,34?

2. What assurance does Jesus give us in verses 32,33?

3. What comfort does Psalm 27:1 give us to help us with anxiety?

4. How can Proverbs 23:18 help us not to despair?

KNOWING *My* HEART

1. How can you put 1 Peter 5:7 into action when you are anxious?

2. How has God affirmed His constant care for you in the past?

3. What current anxieties do you need to cast on Jesus' shoulders?

4. Describe how the Lord will help you in times of despair (Deuteronomy 31:8).

My HEART IN *His* HANDS

"It has been well said that our anxiety does not empty tomorrow of its sorrows, but only empties today of its strength."

—CHARLES H. SPURGEON

Freedom from Anger

The cliché "blowing your top" certainly describes explosive anger. In comic strips, characters in the throes of anger are often shown with steam coming out of their ears. Then there is the "slow burn," which is like coals in a grill glowing until they turn to ashes. By the time the anger is abated, a situation or relationship is ruined. Other forms of anger can also afflict us: resentment, bitterness, hatred, unforgiveness, vengefulness. To which are you most susceptible? For sure, anger ties us in knots and constricts our lives, and may lead to ulcers, high blood pressure, or psychosomatic illnesses. But these are only symptoms of the problem. When we struggle with anger, we need the freeing power of the Holy Spirit to liberate us from our own emotions.

His WORD: Ephesians 4:26,27

KNOWING *His* HEART

1. What is the result of anger that is not dealt with (Psalm 37:8)?

2. What is the danger of allowing anger to linger (Ephesians 4:27)?

3. How should we deal with our anger (Ephesians 4:26)?

4. What instruction does Psalm 4:4 give for dealing with anger?

KNOWING *My* HEART

1. How should we respond when we suffer a hurt or injustice (Proverbs 24:29)?

2. What does Proverbs 25:21 command us to do to our enemies?

3. What advice does James 1:19 gives for controlling our anger?

4. How will you apply these three commands when you are tempted to be angry?

My HEART IN *His* HANDS

"Anger helps straighten out a problem like a fan helps straighten out a pile of papers."
—SUSAN MARCOTTE

Freedom from the Past

Many of us have carried around hurts from the past as open wounds. We may recall these hurts whenever we face difficulties, feel depressed, or encounter opposition. We have no indication that Mary Magdalene let her past defeat her future. In fact, what we see of her is a disciple who faithfully follows Jesus through thick and thin. This is what our freedom is all about. Jesus frees us to do what's right by enabling us to put aside the things in our past that could hinder us. We are God's children, rescued from sin and despair. If God has forgiven and forgotten our sin, we can do no less.

His **WORD:** John 20:1–18

KNOWING *His* HEART

1. How do Mary's actions differ from the disciples' actions (verses 10,11)?

2. Based on this passage, how would you describe Mary's devotion to Jesus?

3. What does 1 Peter 4:1–3 say we should do with our past failures and sins?

4. What does Paul say in 1 Corinthians 15:9,10 about dealing
   with his past?

KNOWING *My* HEART

1. What in your past is keeping you from freely serving God
   wholeheartedly?

2. How can you gain the same devotion to Jesus that Mary Magdalene had?

3. What should we do in serving God (1 Corinthians 15:58)?

4. List two ways you can "stand firm" and experience freedom
   from your past.

My HEART IN *His* HANDS

"*Fret not over the irretrievable, but ever act as if thy life were just
begun.*"
—JOHANN WOLFGANG VON GOETHE

PART 3

Garments of Praise

Do you recall the last time you shopped for a dress to wear to a special occasion, perhaps to a wedding or formal dinner? The clothing racks were likely filled with gorgeous evening gowns, with mannequins posing in sequined dresses. You spot one dress —in your favorite color—with the lines and style that make you look your best. As you try it on, the vision of your body in the flowing gown shimmers in the mirror. Even more surprising, the price of the dress has been cut in half—just in your price range.

With growing excitement, you head for a checkout counter to pay for the dress. As you do, your mind is filled with images of how you will look in the dress at that special occasion.

Now think of putting on the garments of praise. This is like clothing your mind with the most gorgeous gown. It is setting your mind on the grandeur of God's glory and His eternal beauty.

In the Old Testament, the prophet Isaiah warned God's people to turn away from their sin and present themselves completely to God. Isaiah's heart was saddened by the consequences the people were experiencing because of their sinful lifestyle. Isaiah records the words that Jesus would later fulfill: "The LORD has anointed me to provide for those who grieve in Zion—to bestow on them a crown of beauty instead of ashes, the oil of gladness instead of mourning, and a garment of praise instead of a spirit of despair" (Isaiah 61:1,3).

When we place our trust in the Savior, God crowns us with beauty and adorns us in a garment of praise—praise for our marvelous, matchless Lord. Only when our life is yielded to Him are we fulfilling our purpose. Ethel Wilcox tells a story that illustrates this so well.

> In a glass case in one of the palaces in Genoa, Italy, lies the violin of the great violinist, Paganini. It was given to the city to be kept as a treasure, with the instruction that it was never to be played upon again. This instrument, so highly prized that it is kept under guard, at one time uplifted souls of thousands with its matchless music as it yielded itself to the master's touch. But now, not only is its life of usefulness at an end, but it is said it soon may become a heap of dust. The character of the wood is such that having lacked the human touch, the violin has become the victim of tiny insects which are rapidly causing decay.

We are made to be God's instruments of praise. Unless we lift our hearts to praise Him through song, prayer, adoration, and—most importantly—obedience, our lives will deteriorate. Nothing we can do will make our lives more melodious than praising God for who He is and what He has done.

LESSON 11

The Song of a Free Heart

Why do you worship God? We have many reasons for coming before Him, but one motivation for worship is out of joy for what God has done for us. While you are having your quiet time or are sitting in a pew at church, do your thoughts turn to what God has done for you during the week? Do you feel joy at what He has accomplished through your hard times? Are you excited about the blessings He has given you? The Bible gives us an example of one group of people who worshiped God out of joy. Nehemiah and his workers built the wall around Jerusalem to keep their enemies out. Then they took time to give God the praise for their success.

His **WORD:** Nehemiah 12:27–43

KNOWING *His* HEART

1. In what ways did the people worship?

2. Who was involved in the worship?

3. What does Isaiah 12:2–6 tell us about the source of our joy?

4. What action should we take because of our joy (Isaiah 12:4,5)?

KNOWING *My* HEART

1. How has God blessed you in the past week?

2. How can Nehemiah's example help you express your joy about these blessings?

3. Why is it important to include many different kinds of people in corporate worship?

4. How can you express to others the joy that God has given you?

My HEART IN *His* HANDS

"As the people reflect on all God has done, it causes them to rejoice. Let us praise and worship God with singing, for he himself is our song."
—PRAISE AND WORSHIP STUDY BIBLE

The Creativity of Praise

If you watch people in a public place, you will no doubt see individuals wearing all types of clothing—some "dressed for success," others casually attired in T-shirts, shorts, blue jeans, or flannel shirts. The variety of shoes will likely include sneakers, heels, pumps, hiking boots, and sandals. Many people use their creativity to achieve a certain fashion look. Should we be less creative when we put on the garments of praise? Sometimes we get into ruts in our worship and just go through the motions. Other times, we feel we must have a certain style of worship to be effective. But God gives us the freedom to worship Him in unlimited ways.

His **WORD:** Revelation 15:3,4

KNOWING *His* **HEART**

1. How is God worshiped wholeheartedly in 2 Samuel 6:5?

2. What other creative ways to praise are given in Psalm 95:1–7 and Psalm 136?

3. How are we to worship God on the Sabbath (Leviticus 23:3; Psalm 92:1–4)?

4. According to Revelation 15:3,4, how are we to praise God?

KNOWING *My* HEART

1. How should we praise God according to Psalm 150?

2. Use the above list to plan creative ways to praise God this week.

3. How can you incorporate praise in your daily quiet time?

4. What effect will practicing a lifestyle of praise have on your daily life?

My HEART IN *His* HANDS

"God is to be praised because God is God, because of what God is and does, quite apart from what God is and does for me."

—LEANDER E. KECK

LESSON 13

The Joy of Thanksgiving

In the Old Testament times, the Israelites presented thank offerings to the Lord. They brought them to the priest who laid them on the altar. Their offerings represented the gratefulness they felt to the Lord and enabled them to give a public profession of what God had done for them. Too many times, we may offer a quick "thank-you" to God, but our offerings do not require anything of us but a second to throw the sentence skyward. Instead, as we put on garments of praise, we need to offer heartfelt thanksgiving that gives the credit to God. Perhaps if we encounter someone struggling in an area where God has seen us through, we can give testimony of what God has done for us.

His WORD: Psalm 105:1–5

KNOWING *His* HEART

1. What does verse 1 tell us to do in thanking the Lord? Give examples of how we can do this.

2. How does thanksgiving put us into a mindset of rejoicing?

3. Per verse 5, what are some of the wonders has God done for us?

4. Why do we need to thank God for His judgments?

KNOWING *My* HEART

1. What are some of the wonders God has produced in your own life?

2. According to Psalm 106:1, what are two more reasons to be thankful?

3. In what ways do you proclaim to others about the works of God?

4. Make a list of things God has done for you and add to it each week. Thank Him for each one.

My HEART IN *His* HANDS

"Look up on high, and thank the God of all."
—GEOFFREY CHAUCER

Liberating Worship

Sadly, most people who walk into a church sanctuary do not worship God. Instead, their minds are full of everyday concerns and plans for the coming week. They become distracted by items in the bulletin or by what others are doing or wearing. If we are honest, we will admit that we are all susceptible to coming into God's presence—in church, personal devotions, or other worship times—without giving Him honor. Liberating worship is having a mindset that puts God first, intent on giving Him honor and adoration, singing hymns to Him alone. Any other approach to worship easily becomes a desire to be entertained or a preoccupation with personal enrichment. The next time you worship God, put aside everything but God's honor and majesty.

His WORD: Psalm 29:1,2

KNOWING *His* HEART

1. What are the ways we are to worship God as listed in these two verses?

2. What advice does Solomon give for worship (Ecclesiastes 5:1)?

3. What attitude should we have in worship (Habakkuk 2:20)?

4. What does Jesus tell us about worship (John 4:24)?

KNOWING *My* HEART

1. Why do you think true worship of God is so liberating?

2. Think carefully. What are your habits in worship as you enter your church sanctuary?

3. How do these habits hinder or help you worship?

4. In your personal devotions, how much time do you spend being silent before God?

My HEART IN *His* HANDS

"Worship is transcendent wonder."
—THOMAS CARLYLE

LESS⊕N 15

The Act of Worship

Ethel Wilcox is a role model of a woman who truly gave her all to God. In her book, *Power for Christian Living,* she teaches us what we must do to turn our lives over to God. God commands us to present ourselves to Him because of the sacrifice He made for us. Christ gave His all for us; how can we do less? Ethel writes of Romans 12:1, "The literal translation of the word 'present' is 'to stand by the side of.'...So when God asks that we present our bodies a living sacrifice, He is asking that we stand by the side of the altar." That is an act of true worship!

His WORD: Romans 12:1,2

KNOWING *His* HEART

1. According to Hebrews 7:27,28, what kind of sacrifice did Christ make for us?

2. How is offering yourself to God related to your worship of Him (Romans 12:1)?

3. What does God do with us when we present ourselves to Him (Ephesians 2:10)?

4. What is the opposite of doing good works in Christ (Romans 12:2)?

KNOWING *My* HEART

1. How does controlling your body for your own purposes relate to conforming to the world's pattern?

2. Why does Romans 12:1 call offering your body to God *spiritual* worship?

3. What areas of your life have you not offered to God?

4. How will your life change as your present *all* of yourself to God out of love?

My HEART IN *His* HANDS

"*Salvation is the gift of God's Son to us; dedication is the gift of ourselves to God.*"
—ETHEL WILCOX

PART 4

Freedom and Responsibility

Do you remember what it was like to be in school as a child? You sat for long hours in class, listening to teachers droning on and on about topics you may not have cared much about. You completed many assignments that seemed like busywork to you. Sometimes the walls of the classroom seemed like a prison.

Then the bell rang and you ran out the front door of your school. What a feeling! The day was over and you could do what you wanted. You could play with your friends and ride your bike. Perhaps your mother had a snack waiting for you at home.

On the other hand, did you ever play hooky from school? Maybe you pretended you were sick and your mother let you stay home. How did your "lie" make you feel? When the school day ended, you surely didn't have that feeling of joy as when you had completed the hard part of the day and could now enjoy your hours of playtime. Instead, you were stuck inside, eating soup and drinking orange juice. You could probably even hear the children playing outside your window, the ones who had gone to school and were now enjoying games in the yard. The snack your mother had prepared was not offered to you because you needed "healthy" food.

This scenario shows the link between freedom and responsibility. Although we sometimes feel that our work or responsibilities confine our lives, they actually enable us to experience freedom because we are doing what God created us to do—be productive citizens in His kingdom. As we fulfill our God-given responsibilities, God will turn our spiritual "classroom" into a place of joy in service.

Everything God has for us to do is for our enrichment and our learning. As He looks at our lives, He sees what we need and how we can build godly qualities into our lives. That's why He gives us responsibilities. If we just play with our toys—boats, cars, travels, shopping sprees—we will be shallow, dissatisfied, and selfish. What we do can also drain away our freedom by wrapping us up in unhealthy habits and practices.

Children feel better about themselves when they are required to do chores and fulfill responsibilities. We feel better about ourselves when we contribute to the lives of others. Not only that, when we do what God asks us to do, we see miracles and changes in our own lives and in others. What could match the joy of seeing someone place their faith in Christ and experience freedom from sin? This is the result of our faithfulness in witnessing to others.

In our final lessons we will look at the freedom we experience through serving others, the release we have when we manage our money as godly stewards, the importance of fulfilling our political responsibilities, and the liberty of obeying God.

LESSON 16

Freedom Through Service

As Americans living in freedom, we can't imagine what conditions were like for people living in slavery in the Roman empire. Slaves were considered to be mere property, and were forced to do horrific chores without complaining. That's why today's passage in Ephesians is so amazing. Paul tells us that the slave is to serve his master in the same way that a believer serves his Lord—with his whole heart and in humility. That's the kind of service we should offer to God. Our heavenly Father is our Master, but He is no uncaring, cruel taskmaster. We can serve Him with hearts of love and obedience because He always has in mind our ultimate good, and He will walk beside us as we serve Him.

His WORD: Ephesians 6:5–8

KNOWING *His* HEART

1. What do these commandments to slaves teach us about serving others?

2. How does our future reward help us to serve with sincerity and wholeheartedness?

3. Why do you think Psalm 2:11 links serving God with the word "fear"?

4. What is the ultimate depth of service to others (1 John 3:16)?

KNOWING *My* HEART

1. How would you define service to others?

2. Compare your definition with 1 John 3:16. What do you need to adjust in your thinking?

3. In what areas of service are you currently involved?

4. How would you respond if God asked you to serve someone you don't like or at a time that is inconvenient?

My HEART IN *His* HANDS

"In Christian service the branches that bear the most fruit hang the lowest."
—ANONYMOUS

LESS☉N 17

Financial Freedom

Most of us receive frequent applications for new credit cards advertising low interest rates—for a time. Then the rates jump astronomically. High credit-card debt is one way to be a slave to your bills. With a mortgage, car loan, and many other consumer debt obligations, many people worry each month about how to pay all those bills stacked on the table. What's left after paying the bills might be just barely enough to survive. The stress causes tempers to flare and tension to fill the household. Although many live this way, God wants us to live in financial freedom. Take steps today to free yourself from your financial cares! Give your finances over to God and follow the wisdom in His Word.

His WORD: 1 Timothy 6:6–10

KNOWING *His* HEART

1. Describe the bondage mentioned in 1 Timothy 6:9,10.

2. How does Solomon describe the bondage of greed and riches in Ecclesiastes 5:10–12?

3. In what ways is giving the opposite of greediness (2 Corinthians 9:6–8)?

4. What is God's role in our giving (2 Corinthians 9:10,11)?

KNOWING *My* HEART

1. In your monthly budget, how do your interest payments compare to your giving?

2. As described in 2 Corinthians 9:11, how does your giving result in thankfulness?

3. How has God supplied your needs, enabling you to give more to His work?

4. Make a plan to reduce your indebtedness and increase your giving.

My HEART IN *His* HANDS

"Every spending decision is a spiritual decision."
—JAMES RYLE

Political Freedom

Citizenship in a free country is a blessing from God. Our great system of self-government assures every citizen a voice in the affairs of the nation, which enables Christians to bring a heavenly perspective to the earthly realm. When the signers affixed their signatures to the Declaration of Independence, they were well aware that if the colonial cause failed, they would be executed as traitors. They were that dedicated to the cause of freedom. Any less dedication on our part will result in a loss of that precious freedom for which they and thousands of others were willing to die. God wants us to do His will in government. We dare not fail our forefathers, ourselves, and far more importantly, our Lord, to whom this nation was dedicated.

His **WORD:** 2 Samuel 23:3,4

KNOWING *His* **HEART**

1. How does this passage describe the freedom of living under a righteous ruler?

2. What is the difference between living under the rule of the ungodly and of the righteous (Proverbs 29:2)?

56 | MY HEART IN HIS HANDS

3. How might the wisdom in Proverbs 11:11 relate to the importance of active citizenship?

4. What principles for voting do you find in Exodus 18:21?

KNOWING *My* HEART

1. Read 1 Timothy 2:1,2 and make a prayer list for your leaders.

2. As directed by Proverbs 14:18, list some current political issues about which you need to be better informed.

3. How can you get involved with your local politics to help elect godly candidates?

4. What can you do to help others register to vote and get to the polls on election day?

My HEART IN *His* HANDS

"When you become entitled to exercise the right of voting for public officers, let it be impressed upon your mind that God commands you to choose for rulers just men who will rule in the fear of God."

—NOAH WEBSTER

Freedom of Obedience

Imagine a toddler playing in a front yard on a busy street. He would likely have to be frequently pulled back into the safety area. How much better if the yard had a fence. Then the child could safely go wherever he wants to within the yard. In some ways, we act like toddlers in God's "yard." We have a tendency to stray into the "danger zone" of sin. God's rules and commands act like a fence to keep us from harm. Our obedience is the key to our continuing freedom. When we know what our healthy boundaries are, we have freedom in living where God has placed us. The guidelines our Creator gives us allow us to live abundantly and joyfully.

His WORD: Romans 5:18–21

KNOWING *His* HEART

1. Why was the law important in bringing about freedom (Romans 5:20,21)?

2. What was the greatest act of obedience in history (Romans 5:19; Philippians 2:8)?

3. Where does our primary obedience lie (Acts 5:28,29)?

4. What will result from our obedience to God (Romans 16:19)?

KNOWING *My* HEART

1. How does your level of obedience to God compare with Romans 6:15–18?

2. Why do we lose freedom when obeying sin and gain freedom when obeying God?

3. How have you seen this principle at work in your life?

4. In which areas of your life do you need to commit to fully obeying God?

My HEART IN *His* HANDS

"God does not call us to be successful, but to be obedient."
—BILLY GRAHAM

LESSON 20

Freedom of the Abundant Life

Ethel Wilcox lived a life of abundance because of her faith in Christ and her service in His kingdom. She wrote, "Life! Abundant life! This is the kind of life Jesus Christ came to give us... From Genesis to Revelation, against the background of human failures and rebellion, we read of the triumphs of the Lord. 'Victory is of the Lord.'" She was not afraid to put all she had on the line to serve and obey her Lord. And even though she tasted grief in her life, she experienced the joy and freedom of the resurrected Savior. How abundantly do you want to live? How much freedom do you want to taste? The secret lies in placing your life in God's hands and letting Him free you to be what He has planned for you to be.

His WORD: John 10:7–10

KNOWING *His* HEART

1. How are we like sheep and Jesus like the Good Shepherd?

2. Who are the thieves and robbers?

3. What is God's promise in Philippians 4:19?

4. Based on 1 John 5:3–5, describe our victory through obedience.

KNOWING *My* HEART

1. Which of these lessons on freedom means the most to you? Why?

2. How has your attitude toward spiritual freedom been changed through this study?

3. Restate John 8:36 in your own words.

4. How can you integrate 1 Corinthians 9:19 into your ministry to tell others about freedom in Christ?

My HEART IN *His* HANDS

"God is waiting to do our living in and through us; victory is no longer unobtainable. It is truly ours; it is our heritage."

—ETHEL WILCOX

Discussion Guide

T he following pages contain information to help you use the Bible studies in this Guide. If you are using *The Free Heart* lessons as a group study, the answers to the questions will help your facilitator guide the discussion. If you are studying the lessons on your own, refer to the answers after you have finished the lesson.

Answers are given for the first section of questions, called "Knowing HIS Heart." These questions are objective searches through the lesson's Bible passage. The second section, "Knowing MY Heart," are personal application questions and are written to help you use the Bible truths in your everyday life. Therefore, these questions will pertain to your individual situations.

If you are leading a group, work through the first section more thoroughly. Then allow volunteers to give answers to the second section of questions. Some answers may be so personal that your group members will not want to express them aloud. Be sensitive to your group members' feelings in this area.

The Lord bless you are you apply the steps to 'freedom in your life!

Part 1: Spiritual Freedom

LESSON 1: FREELY PROVIDED

1. Through Adam's sin, we inherited judgment, condemnation, and death. Through Christ's death, we can receive justification, grace, righteousness, and eternal life.

2. Through Jesus' death for us, we receive eternal life.

3. Not because of anything we have done, but only because of God's grace in Jesus Christ did He save us and give us life.

4. We received freedom from sin, holiness, and eternal life.

LESSON 2: FREELY FORGIVEN

1. We are slaves to sin, which leads to death, and engage in impurity and wickedness.

2. We are set free from sin and become slaves to righteousness and to God. We experience holiness and eternal life.

3. God has removed them from us and placed them far away. He does this out of His great love.

4. When we sincerely confess our sins to God, He frees us from our guilt and cleanses us.

LESSON 3: THE BOUNDARIES OF FREEDOM

1. God's Word shows us our boundaries, so we must listen to it and do what it says.

2. Looking into God's Word helps us see our sin and failings. If we don't act on what we learn, we will be like that man who looked into the mirror, saw what needed to be fixed, yet turned way and forgot what he saw.

3. We will experience the freedom that obeying God's Word gives us. We will be blessed in whatever we do.

4. If we hold to the teachings in God's Word, we will know the truth and this truth will make us free.

LESSON 4: THE FREEDOM OF GRACE

1. Salvation is a gift of God's grace, which we receive by faith. Our own works cannot earn our salvation.

2. God created us to do good works, which He planned for us long ago.

3. We have this access through Jesus Christ when we place our faith in Him.

4. God's grace is all we need. We are weak, but God is powerful. Therefore, Christ's power is evident in our weakness.

LESSON 5: THE JOY OF SPIRITUAL FREEDOM

1. She followed Him wherever He taught, and gave financial support from her own funds to help with His daily needs.

2. She was still following Him—even to His death on the cross. She was still caring for His needs even though most of the other disciples had deserted Him.

3. She didn't fall away like many others did. She stayed with Him even when it was not popular to follow in His footsteps.

4. She was the first to see Jesus after His resurrection. She was also given the joyful responsibility of telling the disciples that Jesus had risen from the dead.

Part 2: Created to Be Free

LESSON 6: FREE WILL

1. They were impatient, unsubmissive to Moses' leadership, wild and out of control.

2. Each person had to decide whom he would worship—God or the golden idol.

3. He determined that he and his household would serve the Lord.

4. We should submit to God and resist the devil and his temptations.

LESSON 7: FREEDOM IN SUFFERING

1. When we have all kinds of difficulties—whether we are passing through waters, even raging rivers or fire—He will be with us to protect us and help us endure.

2. God was with Paul and the early Christians through their times of suffering. He delivered them from deadly peril and comforted them.

3. We are to comfort others who experience the same kind of suffering we endured, and share with them the comfort we received from God.

4. Remain committed to our faithful God and continue to do good.

LESSON 8: FREEDOM FROM ANXIETY

1. We are not to worry about our life, what we will eat or drink, or what we will wear, or worry about tomorrow.

2. God knows what we need and He will take care of us if we make Him our first priority.

3. God serves as our light and He is our salvation. He is the stronghold of our life so we don't need to fear anything or anyone that comes against us.

4. God assures us that He will give us a future and that He will not allow our hope to be cut off.

LESSON 9: FREEDOM FROM ANGER

1. It turns to wrath and leads to evil.

2. It will give the devil a foothold in our lives.

3. We need to resolve the situation to remove our anger before we go to bed.

4. When we go to bed, we are to search our hearts and be silent so God can speak to us and help us relieve our anger.

LESSON 10: FREEDOM FROM THE PAST

1. After the disciples saw the empty tomb they went home, but Mary stayed by the tomb distraught that Jesus' body was missing.

2. She truly loved the Lord and was brokenhearted that He died. She did all that she could for Jesus before and after His death.

3. We are to abandon our human desires to do evil and instead do the will of God.

4. Paul considered himself the least of the apostles for what he had done in the past. He was saved through the grace of God and accomplished much because of God's Spirit working in him.

Part 3: Garments of Praise

LESSON 11: THE SONG OF A FREE HEART

1. They sang and gave thanks, played musical instruments, listened to choirs, and offered sacrifices.

2. Nehemiah, the Levites, singers, priests, choirs, leaders of Judah, and all the people, including the women and children.

3. Because the Lord is our salvation, He is our strength, our song, and our unending source of joy. We can shout and sing for joy because of the wonderful things He has done for us.

4. We should proclaim His great name to all the world.

LESSON 12: THE CREATIVITY OF PRAISE

1. With songs and with instruments as varied as harps, lyres, tambourines, sistrums, and cymbals.

2. We can worship by singing for joy, shouting, being thankful, praising His majesty and power, bowing in worship, kneeling before Him, submitting to His care. We can also recite many of His great deeds and use repetition for emphasis.

3. We should rest from our work; assemble with other believers; praise God and proclaim His love and faithfulness day and night; make music, sing for joy, and recall what He has done for us.

4. We are to tell God how wonderful He is and what He has done for us in the past, in the present, and in the future.

LESSON 13: THE JOY OF THANKSGIVING

1. We are to tell the nations what God has done. We can tell our coworkers, neighbors, or friends about how God has provided for us spiritually, materially, and eternally.

2. Remembering what God has done fills us with gratitude and joy. Thanksgiving takes our minds off our problems and helps us focus on God's strength and power.

3. He forgives the sins of those who trust in His Son, Jesus Christ. He raised Jesus from the dead. He parted the Red Sea. He provided manna for the people in the wilderness.

4. God is a fair and perfect Judge, so we can thank Him for how He handles all the unfairness in the world. We can trust His judgments.

LESSON 14: LIBERATING WORSHIP

1. Honor the Lord for His glory and strength. Glorify His name and worship His holiness.

2. When we come to worship God, we need to be careful to listen rather than to talk or let our minds wander.

3. We are to come before the Lord in silence because He is holy.

4. We must come before God not just bodily, but with our spirits truly set to worship Him.

LESSON 15: THE ACT OF WORSHIP

1. He offered Himself for our sins. He is perfect forever.

2. We become living sacrifices when we present ourselves completely to God, living a life that is holy and pleasing to God. This is the essence of worshiping Him in our spirits.

3. He enables us to do the good works He prepared for us to do.

4. Being conformed to the pattern of the world.

Part 4: Freedom and Responsibility

LESSON 16: FREEDOM THROUGH SERVICE

1. We must sincerely serve others even under the harshest conditions. We should serve others even when they do not see what we are doing. We are to serve others with the same dedication as when serving God.

2. We know that God can see us at all times. We don't want to be ashamed about how little we have done for others when we come before God, who gave His all for us.

3. We need to be conscious of who God is and serve Him out of awe for His great majesty and power.

4. We are to serve others even if it means sacrificing our own life for them.

LESSON 17: FINANCIAL FREEDOM

1. People who are greedy are ensnared by temptation, and they fall into a harmful trap that leads them away from the faith and into ruin and destruction.

2. The greedy never feel they have enough. They keep consuming more and more as they have the ability to buy, but are never satisfied. Their sleep is disturbed by their worries.

3. Giving pleases God. When we give graciously, God blesses us generously. When we are greedy, we become selfish and isolated.

4. God not only meets our needs but gives us the resources to continue to be generous to others. His harvest will be righteousness. He rewards our generosity with richness in every way possible.

LESSON 18: POLITICAL FREEDOM

1. It is like living under cloudless skies and feeling the sunshine. He brings a freshness to life.

2. Under the righteous ruler, a culture and the people prosper. Under an ungodly ruler, the people are in misery and pain.

3. When citizens are godly, a country is lifted up and succeeds. When the citizens are ungodly, the place in which they live is destroyed.

4. We must elect capable men who fear God and who are honest.

LESSON 19: FREEDOM OF OBEDIENCE

1. The law magnifies our sin so that we see our need for a Savior. But God's grace is greater than sin and death, and brought us righteousness and freedom in Jesus Christ.

2. Jesus was obedient to His Father by coming to earth and dying on a cross so that sinners could be made righteous.

3. Our first allegiance is to God, even if people tell us to do something against His will.

4. Other people will notice our obedience to God, bringing them joy.

LESSON 20: FREEDOM OF THE ABUNDANT LIFE

1. We do not have the ability to run our own lives. We need Jesus to give us guidance, sustenance, and wisdom. He not only gives us spiritual life that is eternal, but He enables us to have a full, abundant life on earth.

2. They are the world, which tempts us to do evil, and the forces of Satan, who want to bind us in sin.

3. He will supply all our needs according to the riches that are in Jesus.

4. When we obey God's commandments, we overcome the world. Our faith in Jesus Christ gives us victory.

Beginning Your Journey of Joy

These four principles are essential in beginning a journey of joy.

One—*God loves you and created you to know Him personally.*

God's Love
"God so loved the world that He gave His one and only Son, that whoever believes in Him shall not perish but have eternal life" (John 3:16).

God's Plan
"Now this is eternal life: that they may know you, the only true God, and Jesus Christ, whom you have sent" (John 17:3).

What prevents us from knowing God personally?

Two—*People are sinful and separated from God, so we cannot know Him personally or experience His love.*

People are Sinful
"All have sinned and fall short of the glory of God" (Romans 3:23).

People were created to have fellowship with God; but, because of our own stubborn self-will, we chose to go our own independent way and fellowship with God was broken. This self-will, characterized by an attitude of active rebellion or passive indifference, is an evidence of what the Bible calls sin.

People are Separated
"The wages of sin is death" [spiritual separation from God] (Romans 6:23).

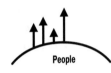

This diagram illustrates that God is holy and people are sinful. A great gulf separates the two. The arrows illustrate that people are continually trying to reach God and establish a personal relationship with Him through our own efforts, such as a good life, philosophy, or religion—but we inevitably fail.

The third principle explains the only way to bridge this gulf...

Three—*Jesus Christ is God's only provision for our sin. Through Him alone we can know God personally and experience His love.*

He Died In Our Place
"God demonstrates His own love toward us, in that while we were yet sinners, Christ died for us" (Romans 5:8).

He Rose from the Dead
"Christ died for our sins...He was buried...He was raised on the third day according to the Scriptures...He appeared to Peter, then to the twelve. After that He appeared to more than five hundred..." (1 Corinthians 15:3–6).

He Is the Only Way to God
"Jesus said to him, 'I am the way, and the truth, and the life; no one comes to the Father but through Me'" (John 14:6).

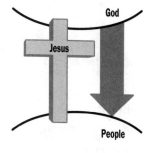

This diagram illustrates that God has bridged the gulf that separates us from Him by sending His Son, Jesus Christ, to die on the cross in our place to pay the penalty for our sins.

It is not enough just to know these three truths...

Four—We must individually receive Jesus Christ as Savior and Lord; then we can know God personally and experience His love.

We Must Receive Christ

"As many as received Him, to them He gave the right to become children of God, even to those who believe in His name" (John 1:12).

We Receive Christ Through Faith

"By grace you have been saved through faith; and that not of yourselves, it is the gift of God; not as a result of works that no one should boast" (Ephesians 2:8,9).

When We Receive Christ, We Experience a New Birth
(Read John 3:1–8.)

We Receive Christ By Personal Invitation

[Christ speaking] "Behold, I stand at the door and knock; if anyone hears My voice and opens the door, I will come in to him" (Revelation 3:20).

Receiving Christ involves turning to God from self (repentance) and trusting Christ to come into our lives to forgive us of our sins and to make us what He wants us to be. Just to agree intellectually that Jesus Christ is the Son of God and that He died on the cross for our sins is not enough. Nor is it enough to have an emotional experience. We receive Jesus Christ by faith, as an act of our will.

These two circles represent two kinds of lives:

Self-Directed Life
S – Self is on the throne
† – Christ is outside the life
● – Interests are directed by self, often resulting in discord and frustration

Christ-Directed Life
† – Christ is in the life and on the throne
S – Self is yielding to Christ
● – Interests are directed by Christ, resulting in harmony with God's plan

Which circle best represents your life?
Which circle would you like to have represent your life?

The following explains how you can receive Christ:

You Can Receive Christ Right Now by Faith Through Prayer
(Prayer is talking with God)

God knows your heart and is not so concerned with your words as He is with the attitude of your heart. The following is a suggested prayer:

> *Lord Jesus, I want to know You personally. Thank You for dying on the cross for my sins. I open the door of my life and receive You as my Savior and Lord. Thank You for forgiving my sins and giving me eternal life. Take control of the throne of my life. Make me the kind of person You want me to be.*

Does this prayer express the desire of your heart?

If it does, I invite you to pray this prayer right now, and Christ will come into your life, as He promised.

How to Know That Christ Is in Your Life

Did you receive Christ into your life? According to His promise in Revelation 3:20, where is Christ right now in relation to you?

Christ said that He would come into your life. Would He mislead you? On what authority do you know that God has answered your prayer? (The trustworthiness of God Himself and His Word.)

The Bible Promises Eternal Life to All Who Receive Christ
"The witness is this, that God has given us eternal life, and this life is in His Son. He who has the Son has the life; he who does not have the Son of God does not have the life. These things I have written to you who believe in the name of the Son of God, in order that you may know that you have eternal life" (1 John 5:11–13).

Thank God often that Christ is in your life and that He will never leave you (Hebrews 13:5). You can know on the basis of His promise that Christ lives in you and that you have eternal life from the very moment you invite Him in. He will not deceive you.

An important reminder...

Feelings Can Be Unreliable
You might have expectations about how you should feel after placing your trust in Christ. While feelings are important, they are unreliable indicators of your sincerity or the trustworthiness of God's promise. Our feelings change easily, but God's Word and His character remain constant. This illustration shows the relationship among **fact** (God and His Word), **faith** (our trust in God and His Word), and our **feelings**.

Fact: The chair is strong enough to support you.

Faith: You believe this chair will support you, so you sit in it.

Feeling: You may or may not feel comfortable in this chair, but it continues to support you.

The promise of God's Word, the Bible—not our feelings—is our authority. The Christian lives by faith (trust) in the trustworthiness of God Himself and His Word.

Now That You Have Entered Into a Personal Relationship With Christ

The moment you received Christ by faith, as an act of your will, many things happened, including the following:

- Christ came into your life (Revelation 3:20; Colossians 1:27).

- Your sins were forgiven (Colossians 1:14).

- You became a child of God (John 1:12).

- You received eternal life (John 5:24).

- You began the great adventure for which God created you (John 10:10; 2 Corinthians 5:17; 1 Thessalonians 5:18).

Can you think of anything more wonderful that could happen to you than entering into a personal relationship with Jesus Christ? Would you like to thank God in prayer right now for what He has done for you? By thanking God, you demonstrate your faith.

To enjoy your new relationship with God...

Suggestions for Christian Growth

Spiritual growth results from trusting Jesus Christ. "The righteous man shall live by faith" (Galatians 3:11). A life of faith will enable you to trust God increasingly with every detail of your life, and to practice the following:

G   *Go* to God in prayer daily (John 15:7).

R   *Read* God's Word daily (Acts 17:11); begin with the Gospel of John.

O   *Obey* God moment by moment (John 14:21).

W   *Witness* for Christ by your life and words (Matthew 4:19; John 15:8).

T   *Trust* God for every detail of your life (1 Peter 5:7).

H   *Holy Spirit*—allow Him to control and empower your daily life and witness (Galatians 5:16,17; Acts 1:8; Ephesians 5:18).

Fellowship in a Good Church

God's Word admonishes us not to forsake "the assembling of ourselves together" (Hebrews 10:25). Several logs burn brightly together, but put one aside on the cold hearth and the fire goes out. So it is with your relationship with other Christians. If you do not belong to a church, do not wait to be invited. Take the initiative; call the pastor of a nearby church where Christ is honored and His Word is preached. Start this week, and make plans to attend regularly.

$\mathcal{R}esources$

My Heart in His Hands: Renew a Steadfast Spirit Within Me. Spring—renewal is everywhere; we are reminded to cry out to God, "Renew a steadfast spirit within me." The first of four books in Vonette Bright's devotional series, this book will give fresh spiritual vision and hope to women of all ages. ISBN 1-56399-161-6

My Heart in His Hands: Set Me Free Indeed. Summer—a time of freedom. Are there bonds that keep you from God's best? With this devotional, a few moments daily can help you draw closer to the One who gives true freedom. This is the second of four in the devotional series. ISBN 1-56399-162-4

My Heart in His Hands: I Delight Greatly in My Lord. Do you stop to appreciate the blessings God has given you? Spend time delighting in God with book three in this devotional series. ISBN 1-56399-163-2

My Heart in His Hands: Lead Me in the Way Everlasting. We all need guidance, and God is the ultimate leader. These daily moments with God will help you to rely on His leadership. The final in the four-book devotional series. ISBN 1-56399-164-0

My Heart in His Hands: Bible Study Guides. Designed to complement the four devotional books in this series, the Bible Study Guides allow a woman to examine God's Word and gain perspective on the issues that touch her life. Each study highlights a biblical character and includes an inspirational portrait

of a woman who served God. Available in 2002:
A Renewed Heart (1-56399-176-4)
A Nurturing Heart (1-56399-177-2)
A Woman's Heart (1-56399-178-0)
A Free Heart (1-56399-179-9)
A Wise Heart (1-56399-180-2)
A Caring Heart (1-56399-181-0)

The Joy of Hospitality: Fun Ideas for Evangelistic Entertaining. Co-written with Barbara Ball, this practical book tells how to share your faith through hosting barbecues, coffees, holiday parties, and other events in your home. ISBN 1-56399-057-1

The Joy of Hospitality Cookbook. Filled with uplifting scriptures and quotations, this cookbook contains hundreds of delicious recipes, hospitality tips, sample menus, and family traditions that are sure to make your entertaining a memorable and eternal success. Co-written with Barbara Ball. ISBN 1-56399-077-6

The Greatest Lesson I've Ever Learned. In this treasury of inspiring, real-life experiences, twenty-three prominent women of faith share their "greatest lessons." Does God have faith- and character-building lessons for you in their rich, heart-warming stories? ISBN 1-56399-085-7

Beginning Your Journey of Joy. This adaptation of the *Four Spiritual Laws* speaks in the language of today's women and offers a slightly feminine approach to sharing God's love with your neighbors, friends, and family members. ISBN 1-56399-093-8

These and other fine products from *NewLife* Publications are available from your favorite bookseller or by calling (800) 235-7255 (within U.S.) or (407) 826-2145, or by visiting www.newlifepubs.com.